PSALM 119:

22 Days of Prayers & Meditations

Queen E. F. Phillips

Books may be ordered through booksellers or by contacting:

QEP Enterprises
P. O. Box 266664
Houston, Texas 77207
queenephillips@aol.com

ISBN: 978-1-304639905

Printed in the United States of America

Table of Contents

Introduction
Day 1 – The Blessed
Day 2 – The Cleansing Way
Day 3 – Deal with Me
Day 4 – Enlarge My Heart
Day 5 – Teach Me
Day 6 – I Will…
Day 7 – Remember
Day 8 – My Portion
Day 9 – I Believe; I Delight
Day 10 – That I May Live and Learn
Day 11 – Help Me Hope!
Day 12 – Your Eternal Word
Day 13 – Sweeter than Honey
Day 14 – Lamp and Light
Day 15 – My Protection
Day 16 – I Am Your Servant
Day 17 – Smile on Me
Day 18 – Truth and Righteousness
Day 19 – Hear My Cry, Lord
Day 20 – Rescue Me
Day 21 – I Love Your Law
Day 22 – Praise and Delight
Keywords and Definitions
Other Keywords and Phrases
From the Author

Introduction

I love this psalm (song)! The writer celebrates the Word of God by expressing his love for and obedience to God's instructions. It is a very lengthy Hebrew acrostic poem. For the 22 consonants in the Hebrew alphabet there are eight (8) verses beginning with that letter. There are a total of 176 verses. Within the psalm, eight (8) Hebrew words for God's Law are used again and again. They are: ***law, testimonies, way, precepts, statues, commandments, judgment and word.***

In the compilation of this devotional, the author provides twenty-two (22) meditations and prayers that correspond with the eight (8) verses within each acrostic beginning with each Hebrew alphabet. Meditation in the

Word of God day and night should be to our delight. This book is inspired for that purpose—to draw us closer to God by thinking on His Word that reveals the importance of us having God's written instructions for living.

This devotional is a practical, simple and easy hands-on resource for new Christian converts and anyone who desires to pray and meditate on the *Excellency* of God's Word, seek Him for knowledge and understanding of His Word and to praise Him for the *Excellency* of His inspired, infallible written Word to us.

Psalm 119: 22-Days of Prayer & Meditations will:

- Inspire and bring awareness to the need to submit to God's instruction.

- Motivate you to seek God's help by praying His Word and applying it to your daily life.

- Manifest the transformational power of God's Word through declaration and meditation.

- Encourage you to believe, stand firmly, declare, and obey God's Word as the "final authority" in every area of life.

Like the psalmist, we all need God's help to remain devoted to Him and to His instructions, which for us, is the Bible. I pray these prayers are a blessing to you, and that they will awaken your hunger and thirst for God's Word, directions and instructions in your life.

Be blessed during your 22 days of prayer and meditation in Psalm 119.

Day 1

The Blessed

Being blessed is not based solely upon external circumstances or material possessions. These verses clearly establish that those who walk (live) in agreement with the Lord's instructions, who observe his witness as faithful and true are blessed (happy, fortunate, to be envied). By seeking and inquiring of the Lord wholeheartedly and craving for Him makes you the "Blessed."

Verses 1-8

1 Blessed are the undefiled in the way,
Who walk in the law of the Lord!
2 Blessed are those who keep His testimonies,
Who seek Him with the whole heart!
3 They also do no iniquity;
They walk in His ways.
4 You have commanded us

To keep Your precepts diligently.
5 Oh, that my ways were directed
To keep Your statutes!
6 Then I would not be ashamed,
When I look into all Your commandments.
7 I will praise You with uprightness of heart,
When I learn Your righteous judgments.

8 I will keep Your statutes;
Oh, do not forsake me utterly

PRAYER

Heavenly Father,

I praise You for providing Your written Word to me. I am blessed because You empower me to walk blamelessly in accordance with Your laws. I desire to keep Your statues and to seek You with all my heart so that I do nothing wrong, but always follow Your ways.

You have commanded me to obey Your precepts and apply Your principles in my life. I confess that my way is not Your way. Help me to consistently and constantly redirect my ways and thoughts to reflect Yours so that I always observe Your statues. I know that doing so will keep me from being ashamed when I consider all Your commands.

Father, I commit myself to You to learn Your righteous laws and to praise You with an upright heart. I will obey Your decrees. I pray that You do not utterly forsake me. I love You and praise Your holy name, Righteous Father. Thank you. In Jesus' Name, I pray. Amen.

Day 2

The Cleansing Way

Whether you are a young man or woman, senior or elder, the Word of God is powerful enough to make your heart pure, if you seek God diligently. There is no magic formula for spiritual cleansing like the laundry cleansers we use to wash away stains in our clothing. In order to experience the cleansing power of God's Word, we must read it, meditate (think) on it, and allow it to soak into our mind and spirit. Your desire to know the Lord is demonstrated by your pursuit of God. As you pray for your personal relationship with God, also pray for the many young men and women who are searching for truth and real meaning in life.

Verses 9 - 16

9 How can a young man cleanse his way?
By taking heed according to Your word.
10 With my whole heart I have sought You;
Oh, let me not wander from Your commandments!
11 Your word I have hidden in my heart,
That I might not sin against You.
12 Blessed are You, O Lord!
Teach me Your statutes.
13 With my lips I have declared
All the judgments of Your mouth.
14 I have rejoiced in the way of Your testimonies,
As much as in all riches.
15 I will meditate on Your precepts,
And contemplate Your ways.
16 I will delight myself in Your statutes;
I will not forget Your word.

PRAYER

Heavenly Father,

Thank you for today and the privilege to pray. Thank you for giving me Your Word to instruct me in your ways so that I know Your will.

Father, I pray that a spirit of obedience to Your Word be released upon all youths and young adults, men and women, that their hearts and minds are cleansed through the sanctifying power of Your Word.

I pray that their hearts are turned toward You, that they hunger and thirst after righteousness that comes through faith in Your Son, Jesus Christ, His blood that was shed and His resurrection. May they know Him as the "Living Word."

Father, I belong to You! Thank You for accepting me into Your family! Let me not wander from Your commandments. I will hide Your Word in my heart so that I don't sin against You.

Teach me Your statues; I will declare all Your judgments.

I commit to rejoicing in the way of Your testimonies as in riches!

Father, I will meditate on Your precepts and have respect to Your ways, which are the paths of life marked out by Your law. Your laws are good for me! I will delight in Your statues. Let me not forget Your Word that it instructs me in righteousness, reproves me in wrongdoing and corrects me. I say, "Yes, Lord!" In Jesus' Name, I pray with thanksgiving. Amen.

Day 3

Deal with Me

It takes complete trust in someone to put yourself under their control. Really, it something no one does willingly. Doing so demonstrates your *total* submission to them; it also gives them permission to treat you any way they choose. You become their servant; the stronger term is *slave.* Truth is, submission is not being under the *control* of another person, but rather implies availability. These verses express the psalmist's availability to God as His servant. He understands that submission, also known as yielding to the Lord is the best decision to secure his life physically, emotionally, and spiritually. As servants of the Most High God, it is to our advantage to say, "Deal with me" knowing we can trust God to do right by us for the better and for our good.

Verses 17-24

17 Deal bountifully with Your servant,
That I may live and keep Your word.
18 Open my eyes, that I may see
Wondrous things from Your law.
19 I am a stranger in the earth;
Do not hide Your commandments from me.
20 My soul breaks with longing
For Your judgments at all times.
21 You rebuke the proud—the cursed,
Who stray from Your commandments.
22 Remove from me reproach and contempt,
For I have kept Your testimonies.
23 Princes also sit and speak against me,
But Your servant meditates on Your statutes.
24 Your testimonies also are my delight
And my counselors.

PRAYER

Heavenly Father,

I reverence You as my sovereign LORD, YAHWEH, Holy, Righteous, Faithful and True! Thank You for this day that gives evidence of Your new mercies and compassion toward me. Thank You for access to Your throne through faith in Jesus Christ, my Savior and Lord.

Lord God, I delight in Your Word and desire to live according to Your instructions. I acknowledge my total dependence upon You. Thank You for redemption and forgiveness of sin through the shed blood of Jesus Christ.

I submit my life totally and willingly to You; I am available to You. Deal generously with me as Your servant that I may live and observe Your word. Lord, open my spiritual eyes and reveal to me the wondrous truths of your Law. I realize that this world is not my home; I am a stranger here. I need to know and understand Your commandments in order to represent You and all that You are in this earth realm. I ask for greater knowledge and revelation of You in Your Word.

I am consumed with knowing You intimately. My soul longs and yearns for Your righteous rulings in my life, home, community, and government.

Father, You rebuke and reprimand the proud— those who stray from Your commands are doomed. Let me not be proud and arrogant by straying from Your commandments. Take away scorn and contempt from me. Remove any and everything that would cause me to disobey Your instructions and be made ashamed and humiliated.

Even if rulers and leaders plot, scheme and slander me, empower Your faithful servant to always meditate on Your law, do what is right, and trust You to fight for me. Your instructions are my delight! I receive Your instructions as my counselors. Whatever problems I face in this life, I find the solutions in Your Word. Help and strengthen me as I commit to applying Your principles in practical living daily. Your Words are spirit and life.

Thank You, Father! I worship You. I seal this prayer in Jesus' Name. Amen.

Day 4

Enlarge My Heart

If you have lived any length of time, you know that there are times when you feel like you are carrying the world on your shoulders. Your heart is too small to carry the baggage. You feel helpless and heavy in your spirit. Sometimes it appears that God is taking a sabbatical. How do you deal with those *weighty* feelings and 'over-sized' emotions? One of the best ways is praying for the revival (refreshing and renewal) of your soul. You can ask for understanding and strength. Always remember to repent and trust God to grant grace and rest. Be assured that He hears you and will enlarge your heart.

Verses 25-32

[25]*My soul clings to the dust;*
Revive me according to Your word.
[26]*I have declared my ways, and You answered me;*
Teach me Your statutes.
[27]*Make me understand the way of Your precepts;*
So shall I meditate on Your wonderful works.
[28]*My soul melts from heaviness;*
Strengthen me according to Your word.
[29]*Remove from me the way of lying,*
And grant me Your law graciously.
[30]*I have chosen the way of truth;*
Your judgments I have laid before me.
[31]*I cling to Your testimonies;*
O Lord, do not put me to shame!
[32]*I will run the course of Your commandments,*
For You shall enlarge my heart.

PRAYER

Heavenly Father,

Hallowed is Your Name. I am in awe of Your majesty! You are great and worthy of all glory and honor.

I bow before You today in submission to Your will and your way. Again I pray in faith, confidence, and expectation of Your promise to hear me when I call unto You. I repent of my sins and ask for forgiveness now so that my prayers are not hindered. Thank You, Father, for being just and faithful to forgive me and cleanse me from all unrighteousness through the precious blood of Jesus Christ of Nazareth.

Father, I delight in Your Word. I need it; I want it! I prostrate myself in Your Presence desperate to hear from You. When I am laid low, revive me by Your word. Lord God, I talk to You about my plans and you answer me, but teach me Your decrees. It is Your purposes and plans that prevail over mine. Make me understand the way of Your precepts so shall I meditate on Your wonderful works.

Father, the cares of this life often cause me to become weary and my soul melts from heaviness; I ask that You strengthen me according to Your word. Keep deceitful and lying ways far from me and favor me with Your law.

Lord God, I choose the way of truth. Your judgments I have laid before me to walk therein. Help me to hold fast to Your testimonies, O LORD, do not put me to shame as I am called by Your Name. I will run in step with Your commandments, realizing it is You who enlarges my heart and broadens my understanding.

Oh! How I praise You! I worship You in spirit and in truth. You alone are God. Thank You for this privilege and access to Your grace through Jesus Christ, my Redeemer and Lord.

I pray this prayer with thanksgiving. I seal it in the Name of Jesus, the blood and the Holy Spirit. Amen.

Day 5

Teach Me

You have probably heard the adage, *knowledge is power*. Who does not want power? Good news is that God's power is available to anyone who will pursue Him. As you earnestly pursue Him, power is available. The knowledge that you desire, and the power that is available comes from God's Spirit and His Word. The simplest prayers are these: Teach me, Lord; give me understanding; make me walk…; incline my heart; turn away my eyes; establish Your word; revive me. Ultimately, your prayer of petition is to ask God to give you experiences that will teach you His way of doing things and enable you to follow through on what He teaches you.

Verses 33-40

33 Teach me, O Lord, the way of Your statutes,
And I shall keep it to the end.
34 Give me understanding, and I shall keep Your law;
Indeed, I shall observe it with my whole heart.
35 Make me walk in the path of Your
commandments,
For I delight in it.
36 Incline my heart to Your testimonies,
And not to covetousness.
37 Turn away my eyes from looking at worthless
things,
And revive me in Your way.
38 Establish Your word to Your servant,
Who is devoted to fearing You.
39 Turn away my reproach which I dread,
For Your judgments are good.
40 Behold, I long for Your precepts;
Revive me in Your righteousness.

PRAYER

Heavenly Father,

You are great and mighty, awesome in all Your doings! Holy, just, and righteous You are. Thank

You for this new day and the privilege to pray to You in the Name of Jesus Christ, Your Son, our Savior and Lord.

Father, Your ways are awesome! Teach ME, O LORD, Your laws; keeping, observing and obeying them will be my rewards. Give me understanding so that I will have no excuse for not keeping Your law. I will observe Your law completely with my whole heart.

Guide me in the path of Your commandments because I take pleasure in them; Your commandments are my delight. Bend and turn my heart toward Your instructions, LORD, and not toward selfish gain and vain ambitions.

Father, turn my eyes away from worthless things that add no value to my life or Your purpose. Give me life with Your ways.

I am Your servant, Father. I worship You in spirit and in truth. Fulfill Your promise, which You made to all who reverently worship You. Let me not bring disgrace to Your name. Help me abandon any shameful ways for Your laws and regulations are good. Father, I long to obey Your commandments! Renew, revive and restore my life with Your goodness and righteousness.

Thank you, Holy Father!

I seal this prayer in the Excellent Name of Jesus the Christ and His Blood, and the Spirit of Truth with thanksgiving. Amen.

Day 6

I Will…

Have you ever made a promise but could not keep it? In this life, things happen that will keep you from fulfilling the promises you had every intention of keeping. Thankfully, God is incapable of breaking His promises to us. Making promises is a serious matter and God takes it serious. In the verses below, the psalmist makes several promises to the Lord. However, notice that his "I wills" (promises) are contingent upon his relationship to God and His word, ordinances, precepts, testimonies, and statues. Like the psalmist, we too should commit to making and keeping our promises to Him. Understand though, only God can enable and empower you to fulfill your "I wills…"

Verses 41 – 48

41 Let Your mercies come also to me, O Lord—
Your salvation according to Your word.
42 So shall I have an answer for him who reproaches me,
For I trust in Your word.
43 And take not the word of truth utterly out of my mouth,
For I have hoped in Your ordinances.
44 So shall I keep Your law continually,
Forever and ever.
45 And I will walk at liberty,
For I seek Your precepts.
46 I will speak of Your testimonies also before kings,
And will not be ashamed.
47 And I will delight myself in Your commandments,
Which I love.
48 My hands also I will lift up to Your commandments,
Which I love,
And I will meditate on Your statutes.

PRAYER

Heavenly Father,

You are great and mighty! Holy and righteous is Your Name. Thank You for this new day and the privilege to pray to You in the Name of Jesus Christ, Your Son, my Savior and Lord.

Father, I confess that I need Your love to flow continuously through me. Give me Your love. Let Your grace come to me and Your salvation that I will effectively communicate Your answer from Your Word to those who taunt and ridicule me. I trust in Your word.

I pray that Your word of truth is always in my mouth; for my hope is in Your ordinances. I shall keep Your law continuously, forever and ever. I decree and declare that I will walk in liberty as I seek Your precepts and am empowered to live accordingly.

I will speak of Your testimonies before leaders, kings and government officials, and will not be ashamed to call upon You. I will boldly declare that You are the only true and living God.

Father, I will delight myself in Your commandments, which I love. I will lift my hands up to You in surrender because I love You. I will meditate on Your statues. Help me, God!

Thank you, Holy Father! Oh! How I worship You! I seal this prayer in the Excellent Name of Jesus the Christ and His Blood, and the Spirit of Truth with thanksgiving. Amen.

Day 7
Remember

I admit, it is difficult for me to remember names. I try very hard, but I forget very quickly. Amazingly, I can remember dreams from many years ago that were given by God. How good is your memory? Are you good at remembering names and memorable events in life? Is it easier for you to remember good times or bad times? Our finite minds and limitations make remembering difficult in many instances. However, I am so grateful that God remembers His word to us. On the other hand, I am grateful that He does not remember my sins! Moreover, I am thankful that He touches my mind so that I can remember His name even in my dark (night) times. When I remember His goodness and how much He loves me, I am comforted. I live in expectation and anticipation of the manifestation of His Word in my life, situations, and all that concerns me.

Verses: 49-56

49 *Remember the word to Your servant,*
Upon which You have caused me to hope.
50 *This is my comfort in my affliction,*
For Your word has given me life.
51 *The proud have me in great derision,*
Yet I do not turn aside from Your law.
52 *I remembered Your judgments of old, O Lord,*
And have comforted myself.
53 *Indignation has taken hold of me*
Because of the wicked, who forsake Your law.
54 *Your statutes have been my songs*
In the house of my pilgrimage.
55 *I remember Your name in the night, O Lord,*
And I keep Your law.
56 *This has become mine,*
Because I kept Your precepts.

PRAYER

Heavenly Father,

Great and mighty You are! Holy and righteous is Your Name. Thank You for this new day, I rejoice in it and the privilege to pray to You in the Name of Jesus Christ, Your Son, our Savior and Lord.

Your word is the foundation of my hope as Your servant. Whatever you have spoken gives me a reason to expect Your word to manifest in my personal life, ministry, and in the earth realm. This is what comforts and consoles me in times of adversity and affliction. Your word gives life to me. Thank You, Father, for Your word.

Father, You know and see the arrogant who scorn Your people for being followers of Your Son, but let me not turn away from Your age-old rulings; instead, let me continue to stand steadfast and take comfort in Your law. Let me not be comfortable and compromise with the wicked, but stir up indignation and anger because of those who abandon your instruction.

Father, I pray that my anger stirs me to be a better witness, live a better life, and hold fast to the faith of my profession.

Lord, put songs of praise in my heart so that Your statues resound wherever I live. Lord, I vow to remember Your name at nighttime, even during the night seasons of my life. Help me to keep Your instructions. Let this be my practice as I guard Your precepts in all that I do and say. I am Your servant who obeys Your commands because I love You, and more importantly, because You love me.

Thank You for everything. I give You all praise and glory, forever and ever.

I seal this prayer in the Excellent Name of Jesus the Christ and His Blood, and the Spirit of Truth with thanksgiving. Amen.

Day 8

My Portion

Having a good, healthy relationship with someone makes life a whole lot better. Do you agree? Are you blessed to have someone you can share your innermost thoughts and express your feelings without being judged or condemned? Do you feel appreciated and loved in spite of your faults and weaknesses? Are you one hundred percent confident that you have the support of family and friends? Better yet, can they depend on you to support them during life's challenging times? You do know that life is filled with transitions, right? This is why it is so important to have a relationship with Jesus Christ and say as the psalmist, *"Lord, you are my portion."* When you really think about God's unconditional love, grace and mercy, you will realize that having a relationship with Him makes your life worth living.

Verses: 57-64

[57]You are my portion, O Lord;
I have said that I would keep Your words.
[58]I entreated Your favor with my whole heart;
Be merciful to me according to Your word.
[59]I thought about my ways,
And turned my feet to Your testimonies.
[60]I made haste, and did not delay
To keep Your commandments.
[61]The cords of the wicked have bound me,
But I have not forgotten Your law.
[62]At midnight I will rise to give thanks to You,
Because of Your righteous judgments.
[63]I am a companion of all who fear You,
And of those who keep Your precepts.
[64]The earth, O Lord, is full of Your mercy;
Teach me Your statutes.

PRAYER

Heavenly Father,

Oh! How I reverence You, my Creator. Great and Holy is Your name in all the earth! You alone are worthy of all praise, honor and glory.

You O LORD are my portion, my possession. I have promised that I would obey Your words. Today and henceforth, I will seek Your face with all my heart. I ask for Your graciousness toward me according to Your promise. I have and do consider my ways and have turned my steps toward Your statues. I repent for not following Your way.

Father, I hasten and will not hesitate in obeying Your commands. I will not forget Your laws even if the wicked attempt to hold me captive. In the night watches, in the night seasons of my life, and even at midnight, I will give thanks to You for Your righteous laws.

I reverence You. I worship You; I join myself in relationship as friends to all who fear You and follow Your prescribed principles.

Thank You, Father, that the earth is filled with Your love! O LORD, *teach me how to demonstrate Your love. Teach me Your decrees that I may represent You in a more excellent way while living on this earth.*

I seal this prayer in the Excellent Name of Jesus the Christ and His Blood, and the Spirit of Truth with thanksgiving. Amen.

Day 9

I Believe; I Delight

Life's experiences have a way of teaching us, at least they should. Trials and tribulations should come as no surprise to the believer. God will use them to teach and develop us; therefore, we should always believe His Word and delight in His teachings. When we do, we are able to see from His perspective and declare that in spite of opposition and affliction God is good and His Word is good for us.

Verses: 65-72

65 You have dealt well with Your servant,
O Lord, according to Your word.
66 Teach me good judgment and knowledge,
For I believe Your commandments.
67 Before I was afflicted I went astray,

But now I keep Your word.
68 *You are good, and do good;*
Teach me Your statutes.
69 *The proud have forged a lie against me,*
But I will keep Your precepts with my whole heart.
70 *Their heart is as fat as grease,*
But I delight in Your law.
71 *It is good for me that I have been afflicted,*
That I may learn Your statutes.
72 *The law of Your mouth is better to me*
Than thousands of coins of gold and silver.

PRAYER

Heavenly Father,

I worship You and praise Your holy name! Thank You for Your goodness!

I ask as the psalmist, Do good and be favorable to Your servant according to Your word, O LORD.

Teach me good judgment and knowledge. I believe Your commands, delight and desire to know Your will.

Before my afflictions, troubles and hardships, I strayed from You; now I obey Your word. Forgive me, Father.

You are good and whatever You do is good! Teach me, Lord, Your decrees. Do not let me be persuaded to disobey Your laws because of lies and ill-spoken words against me. My delight is in You and Your laws.

Lord, thank You that You allow hardships, challenges, and sufferings so that I might come closer to You, believe Your word, trust You, and learn Your decrees. I recognize that the law from Your mouth is more precious and valuable to me than thousands of pieces of silver and gold, or all the money in the world.

Thank You for being a good God, my Father who loves me unconditionally.

I seal this prayer in the Excellent Name of Jesus the Christ and His Blood, and the Spirit of Truth with thanksgiving. Amen.

Day 10

That I May Live and Learn

I am amazed by our CREATOR! Do you know that all of creation testifies of His wisdom? The world was framed by His spoken word! He has made everything to glorify Himself, especially mankind. Because He made and fashioned us, He knows *everything* about us. This is too wonderful for my finite mind to fully conceive, but how I want to live in Him and learn of Him. Moreover, He desires that we learn and understand our relationship to Him. Our relationship with Him is broken if there is no reverence. Our reverence is acknowledged by our trust and dependence upon Him in every area of life. Our life is a display of our hope in His merciful kindness and faithfulness.

Verses: 73-80

73 Your hands have made me and fashioned me;
Give me understanding, that I may learn Your commandments.

74 Those who fear You will be glad when they see me,
Because I have hoped in Your word.
75 I know, O Lord, that Your judgments are right,
And that in faithfulness You have afflicted me.
76 Let, I pray, Your merciful kindness be for my comfort,
According to Your word to Your servant.
77 Let Your tender mercies come to me, that I may live;
For Your law is my delight.
78 Let the proud be ashamed,
For they treated me wrongfully with falsehood;
But I will meditate on Your precepts.
79 Let those who fear You turn to me,
Those who know Your testimonies.
80 Let my heart be blameless regarding Your statutes,
That I may not be ashamed.

PRAYER

Heavenly Father,

You are great and mighty! Thank You for this new day; I rejoice in it! Thank You for the privilege of praying to You in the Name of Jesus Christ, Your Son, my Savior and Lord.

Because Your hands have made me and established me; cause me to understand. I want to live and learn about Your righteous judgments, precepts, and commandments. Teach me so that I may learn all that You want to reveal to me.

Let my life be an example and encouragement to other worshippers that they will see and be glad because I hope in Your word.

LORD, I trust You completely! Your judgments are right. In Your faithfulness and trustworthiness You afflicted me. Thank You for being faithful to me.

Let Your steadfast and unconditional love be my comfort as You promised. Let Your mercies come to me that I may live for Your law is my delight. Father, let the arrogant be put to shame because they have wronged me with lies. I declare, I will meditate on Your precepts. Let those who reverence You turn to me. Let those who know and understand Your testimonies walk in agreement with Your law. Lord God, I pray that my heart be blameless in Your statues so that I am not ashamed.

Thank You for everything. I give You all praise and glory, forever and ever. I seal this prayer in the Excellent Name of Jesus the Christ and His Blood, and the Spirit of Truth with thanksgiving. Amen.

Day 11

Help Me Hope!

Have you ever prayed, "Lord, when will You…?" I have lots of times and God has not rebuked me for asking. Why is that? He knows that my asking means I am looking for Him to help me. Asking *when* expresses my expected manifestation of God's promises. Although you may be asking *when*, just make sure you do not forget God's Word provides the comfort you need to wait patiently for Him to rescue you. He will help you hope in His Word. Sure, your emotions may be fighting against your faith, and your enemies may be ganging up on you in an attempt to bring an end to your life, but I declare unto you that God's Word has resurrection power. It will revive you! When all is said and done, you will bear witness to God's loving-kindness that is better than life.

Verses: 81-88

81 My soul faints for Your salvation,
But I hope in Your word.
82 My eyes fail from searching Your word,
Saying, "When will You comfort me?"
83 For I have become like a wineskin in smoke,
Yet I do not forget Your statutes.
84 How many are the days of Your servant?
When will You execute judgment on those who persecute me?
85 The proud have dug pits for me,
Which is not according to Your law.
86 All Your commandments are faithful;
They persecute me wrongfully;
Help me!
87 They almost made an end of me on earth,
But I did not forsake Your precepts.
88 Revive me according to Your loving-kindness,
So that I may keep the testimony of Your mouth.

PRAYER

Heavenly Father,

You alone are worthy of all praise, honor and glory. Great and Holy is Your name in all the earth! Oh! How we reverence You, our Creator.

My soul faints and longs for Your salvation! Deliver me; rescue me, I pray. I hope in Your promise.

My expectation is in Your word; I long to see its manifestation in my life and in the earth realm. Lord, when will You comfort me in my troubles and hardships?

Although I am desperately waiting and exhausted, feeling dried out from my heated situation, I have not forgotten Your statues. In my desperation I cry, "Lord, how much longer before You execute justice against the arrogant who have dug pits for me and all who oppose Your law? They are deceitful and behave deceitfully.

Father, all Your commands are faithful. Help me, Lord, to hope patiently in You! They have almost destroyed me, but I have not forsaken Your precepts. Keep me; revive me according to Your steadfast and loyal love. Preserve me that I may heed the testimony from Your mouth.

Thank You for hearing and answering my heart's cry for help. I give You all praise and glory, forever and ever.

I seal this prayer in the Excellent Name of Jesus the Christ and His Blood, and the Spirit of Truth with thanksgiving. Amen.

Day 12

Your Eternal Word

Matthew 24:35 records Jesus' saying, *"Heaven and earth shall pass away, but my words shall not pass away."* People, places, and things all change at some point or in some way in this life. We may or may not like the changes, but in some cases there is nothing we can do about it. For example, the weather changes; the seasons change, and certainly as we age, our physical body changes. Sometimes our perspectives and beliefs change. Some change is considered good for us and some may not be so good for us. I am so thankful that God's Word will never change. It is eternal! Remember, you will see change happening all around you. It may be good or not *feel* so good, but rest assuredly, God is faithful and His Word is forever established and settled in heaven. This truth should keep us grounded in the Word of God.

Verses 89 - 96

89 Forever, O Lord,
Your word is settled in heaven.
90 Your faithfulness endures to all generations;
You established the earth, and it abides.
91 They continue this day according to Your
ordinances,
For all are Your servants.
92 Unless Your law had been my delight,
I would then have perished in my affliction.
93 I will never forget Your precepts,
For by them You have given me life.
94 I am Yours, save me;
For I have sought Your precepts.
95 The wicked wait for me to destroy me,
But I will consider Your testimonies.
96 I have seen the consummation of all perfection,
But Your commandment is exceedingly broad.

PRAYER

Heavenly Father,

You are great; You are holy. Your name is to be exalted in all the earth! You alone are worthy of all praise, honor and glory. Oh! How we reverence You, our Creator.

O YAHWEH, Your word is forever settled in heaven; it stands firms. Your faithfulness endures from a generation to a generation. You have established the earth and it stands by the power of Your word.

Your rules and ordinances uphold all things. I acknowledge that I would have perished in my distress if Your law had not been my delight.

I vow to never forget Your requirements and principles because I am alive through them. I am yours! The wicked desires my destruction, but my focus is on Your instructions. Rescue me because I seek Your precepts.

Father, I recognize everything has limitations no matter how perfect and complete they are, but Your commandments have no limits. Your word is the final authority.

I give You all praise and glory, forever and ever.

I seal this prayer in the Excellent Name of Jesus the Christ and His Blood, and the Spirit of Truth with thanksgiving. Amen.

Day 13

Sweeter than Honey

Are your taste buds working properly? Do you have an appetite for certain cuisine at various times? For example, during the summer, I crave chilled fruit, especially watermelon, smoothies, key lime pie, coconut meringue pie, fresh salads and ice-cold flavored drinks to endure this Texas heat. Then when winter comes, I please my taste buds and satisfy my cravings with a good bowl of hot chili or homemade vegetable soup. You get the idea, right? We eat the foods we love and that will satisfy our appetite at any given time. How about your love and appetite for the Word? It should satisfy your cravings at all times and seasons. Can we say like the psalmist that God's Word is sweeter than honey?

Verses 97 – 104

97 Oh, how I love Your law!
It is my meditation all the day.
98 You, through Your commandments, make me wiser than my enemies;
For they are ever with me.
99 I have more understanding than all my teachers,
For Your testimonies are my meditation.
100 I understand more than the ancients,
Because I keep Your precepts.
101 I have restrained my feet from every evil way,
That I may keep Your word.
102 I have not departed from Your judgments,
For You Yourself have taught me.
103 How sweet are Your words to my taste,
Sweeter than honey to my mouth!
104 Through Your precepts I get understanding;
Therefore I hate every false way.

PRAYER

Heavenly Father,

Oh! How I reverence You, the Creator. Holy is Your name in all the earth! You alone are worthy of all praise, honor, and glory.

O! How I love Your law; I meditate on it all day. Your commandments make me wiser than my enemies. I pray that because You give me understanding of Your commandments, I will not be overtaken my foes nor deceived by the enemy's tactics. Let me continue to keep and understand Your instructions so that I might teach others Your way.

Father, I resolve with Your help, I will keep my feet from every evil way in order to observe Your word with my whole heart. Let me not turn away from Your rulings because You have instructed me and guides me daily in agreement with Your word.

Your promises are sweet to my tongue, truly sweeter than honey in my mouth! I love Your law! Lord, from Your precepts I gain understanding; this is why I hate very false way. Let me not be persuaded to follow after the false way, only Your way, which assures me of an expected end.

Thank You, Father, for Your goodness and the instructions You give so that I can walk in accordance with Your word and love You with my whole heart, soul, mind, and strength.

I seal this prayer in the Excellent Name of Jesus the Christ and His Blood, and the Spirit of Truth with thanksgiving. Amen.

Day 14

Lamp and Light

Have you ever walked into a dark room without stumbling into objects? Although you may be familiar with the surroundings, your safety is still at risk. Have you ever had to walk down a country dirt road with no street lights? I have. I am a country girl and I can tell you from experience, it was a fearful journey even if you had a flashlight. Having a lamp or light to see your way in darkness with each step you take will keep you from stumbling or walking into objects. Your safety is God's concern. Your safe place in this dark world is in the Word of God. God's Word will shine brightly, but you have to use it to guide you as you travel life's journey.

Verses: 105-112

105 *Your word is a lamp to my feet*
And a light to my path.
106 *I have sworn and confirmed*
That I will keep Your righteous judgments.
107 *I am afflicted very much;*
Revive me, O Lord, according to Your word.
108 *Accept, I pray, the freewill offerings of my mouth,*
O Lord,
And teach me Your judgments.
109 *My life is continually in my hand,*
Yet I do not forget Your law.
110 *The wicked have laid a snare for me,*
Yet I have not strayed from Your precepts.
111 *Your testimonies I have taken as a heritage forever,*
For they are the rejoicing of my heart.
112 *I have inclined my heart to perform Your statutes*
Forever, to the very end.

PRAYER

Heavenly Father,

You alone are worthy of all praise, honor, and glory.
Oh! How I reverence You, my Creator.
Your word is a lamp to my feet and a light that
provides guidance and directions for my path in life.

Father, I vow to keep your righteous rules although my troubles and struggles are sometimes great. Give me life, O Lord according to your word!
Accept my freewill offerings of praise and teach me your rules. My life is continuously in danger, but I will remember your law. Although the wicked lay a snare for me, help me not to stray from your precepts and principles because they preserve and protect me. Your testimonies are my heritage forever; they are the joy of my heart. Lord, I turn my heart to perform Your statues forever, to the end.
Thank you for empowering me to stand firmly on the foundation of Your word.
I seal this prayer in the Excellent Name of Jesus the Christ and His Blood, and the Spirit of Truth with thanksgiving. Amen.

Day 15
My Protection

Do you recall any dangerous experiences in your life? What kind of impact did facing danger have on you? While we live on this earth, we may find ourselves in dangerous situations because evil is always present. There is much controversy about gun control and the right to bear arms in our society; some favor it and some do not. Yet, others stand firm on their belief that they have the right carry arms. Safety is a major concern in society especially with the increase in violent crimes. Unfortunately, man has no real solution to eliminate the threat of evil and secure our safety in this world. The expressed concerns of the psalmist speaks to us about the danger of being surrounded by evil and evildoers. The safest place to be is in Christ. We should declare as the psalmist, *"Lord, You are my hiding place and my shield."* In other words, the Lord is my protection and my covering. He alone can protect us from the evil one and evildoers. To guarantee my protection, I will keep the commandments of my God!

Verses: 113-120

113 *I hate the double-minded,*
But I love Your law.
114 *You are my hiding place and my shield;*
I hope in Your word.
115 *Depart from me, you evildoers,*
For I will keep the commandments of my God!
116 *Uphold me according to Your word, that I may live;*
And do not let me be ashamed of my hope.
117 *Hold me up, and I shall be safe,*
And I shall observe Your statutes continually.
118 *You reject all those who stray from Your statutes,*
For their deceit is falsehood.
119 *You put away all the wicked of the earth like dross;*
Therefore I love Your testimonies.
120 *My flesh trembles for fear of You,*
And I am afraid of Your judgments.

PRAYER

Heavenly Father,

You are great! There is none like You. Thank You for this new day of mercies. Great is Your faithfulness unto me. I shall rejoice in Your everlasting love. I am grateful for the privilege of prayer.

I love Your law. Lord, let it be the governor of my thoughts so that I am not consumed by meaningless and unrighteous thoughts. I pray that vanity does not control my thought life.

Lord, You are my hiding place, my refuge, protection, and shield. You cover me; therefore, I hope in Your promise. Help me, Lord, not to walk the path of evildoers. My choice, by Your grace, is to live in obedience to Your commandments. You are my God. Uphold me; sustain with the supernatural, active power of your Word so that I may live. I pray, let me not be ashamed of my hope, which is in Your promises. I am confident that if You hold me up, if you sustain me, I shall be safe. I will respect and reverence Your statues always.

Let me not err from Your statues and be brought down by deceitfulness and falsehood. You reject all who disobey Your statues and stray from your decrees.

I tremble in fear of You; I stand in awe of Your regulations. You are my God!

Thank you for empowering me to stand firmly on the foundation of Your Word.

I seal this prayer in the Excellent Name of Jesus the Christ and His Blood, and the Spirit of Truth, with thanksgiving. Amen.

Day 16
I Am Your Servant

How do you treat your waitresses and waiters who serve your table when you dine out? It can say a lot about your attitude toward servanthood. Servants are not always esteemed in our society. Instead, they are referred to as the *hired help* or other belittling names. The word *servant* is used over and over in this psalm. There is no mistake about the psalmist identifying himself as a servant.

During Jesus' earthly ministry He taught the disciples by demonstration what the role and attitude of a servant should be.

Do you identify yourself as a servant of God? If so, what kind of relationship do you have with your Master? Can He trust you to do what is fair and right? More importantly, you can depend on your Master to deal with you mercifully and to treat you fairly and right. To be honest, our Master treats us much better than we deserve. Would you agree? We should be extremely grateful because God does not belittle His servants. Instead, we can ask Him for help, especially in our time of need, and He will act on our behalf.

Verses: 121-128

121 I have done justice and righteousness;
Do not leave me to my oppressors.
122 Be surety for Your servant for good;
Do not let the proud oppress me.
123 My eyes fail from seeking Your salvation
And Your righteous word.
124 Deal with Your servant according to Your mercy,
And teach me Your statutes.
125 I am Your servant;
Give me understanding,
That I may know Your testimonies.
126 It is time for You to act, O Lord,
For they have regarded Your law as void.
127 Therefore I love Your commandments
More than gold, yes, than fine gold!
128 Therefore all Your precepts concerning all things
I consider to be right;
I hate every false way.

PRAYER

Heavenly Father,

You are the Most High and Holy God. I reverence you. Thank You for this new day, we rejoice in it, and the privilege to pray to You in the Name of Jesus Christ, Your Son, our Savior and Lord.

Father, I ask that you have mercy on me and not leave me to the mercy of my enemies, for I have done what is just and right. Don't let the arrogant oppress me, bless me indeed. I am waiting with great expectation to see your salvation. I hope in your rescue and to see your promise fulfilled.

I am committed to being your servant; deal with me in unfailing and unconditional love. Teach me your decrees. I ask for discernment so that I will understand your laws.

I pray for the manifestation of your justice against the evildoers and all who violate your instructions. Lord God, I really love your commands more than the finest gold. I esteem each of your commandments everything you do right and just, help me to follow you in all things and hate every false way.

Thank you for revealing truth and instructing me in righteousness through your word.

I seal this prayer in the Excellent Name of Jesus the Christ and His Blood, and the Spirit of Truth, with thanksgiving. Amen.

Day 17

Smile on Me

What is it about a smile that can make a person's day? I am not going to share any clinical details or try to explain the physiological and psychological effects of smiling; I am not qualified to do so. However, I am sure that at some point you have experienced the positive effects of a smile. Smiles give the impression that all is well, even when it is not well. Smiles are expressions of happiness, delight, friendliness, joy, pleasure, excitement. Smiles are inviting gestures of praise.

Do you know you can ask God to smile on you? The psalmist did just that in these verses. These lyrics express the sentiment of the psalmist's desire and praise for God's words. Amazingly, reading and meditating on God's word will evoke such excitement and contentment that before you know it you are literally smiling. When others reject God's love and disobey His laws, does it break your heart? It is the opportune time for you to pray for them to receive the light of God's Word. When His word enters your heart and penetrate your spirit it illuminates your mind and enables you see from a different perspective. You look through lens of faith. God's word can make your day and cause tears of joy to run down your face because He is smiling on you. Go ahead. Ask Him.

Verses: 129-136

129 Your testimonies are wonderful;
Therefore my soul keeps them.
130 The entrance of Your words gives light;
It gives understanding to the simple.
131 I opened my mouth and panted,
For I longed for Your commandments.
132 Look upon me and be merciful to me,
As Your custom is toward those who love Your name.
133 Direct my steps by Your word,
And let no iniquity have dominion over me.
134 Redeem me from the oppression of man,
That I may keep Your precepts.
135 Make Your face shine upon Your servant,

And teach me Your statutes.
136 *Rivers of water run down from my eyes,*
Because men do not keep Your law.

PRAYER

Heavenly Father,

Thank You for this new day and for your compassions that never fail. You are faithful and true. I appreciate the privilege of talking to You; thank you

How wonderful are your testimonies; therefore, my soul shall follow them wholeheartedly.

Your words are a doorway that lets in light; they give me understanding so that I may know in simplicity what you require and expect. I pray for your continuous light to shine in my heart. I yearn and pant with expectation for your commands. I love you with all my heart, mind and soul.

Guide my steps by Your word, I pray. I ask do not let evil overcome me. Ransom me from the oppression of evil people. Set me free from myself so that I can obey Your commandments. Look upon me with Your unconditional love and teach me Your decrees. I want to know you.

I cry because I am saddened when people disobey your instructions. I pray that they would hear you and follow your commands. Let me experience comfort that comes from reading Your Word. Smile on me and turn my tears of sadness into joy as I embrace Your Presence.

Thank you for revealing truth and instructing me in righteousness through your word.

I seal this prayer in the Excellent Name of Jesus the Christ and His Blood, and the Spirit of Truth, with thanksgiving. Amen.

Day 18

Truth and Righteousness

Does it upset you when people do not follow the Lord's teaching? It should to an extent because you know God is righteous and faithful, that His rulings are just and that He wants everyone to experience salvation through faith in His Son Jesus Christ. Although some people will not receive Him, and may despise you, remain true to Him. Although it may appear that trouble and anguish have overtaken you, do not forget His principles. Always stand firmly in your conviction that God is trustworthy, His teachings are true and His rules are just. Ask Him for understanding and you will live.

Verses: 137-144

137 Righteous are You, O Lord,
And upright are Your judgments.
138 Your testimonies, which You have commanded,
Are righteous and very faithful.
139 My zeal has consumed me,
Because my enemies have forgotten Your words.
140 Your word is very pure;
Therefore Your servant loves it.
141 I am small and despised,
Yet I do not forget Your precepts.
142 Your righteousness is an everlasting righteousness,
And Your law is truth.
143 Trouble and anguish have overtaken me,
Yet Your commandments are my delights.
144 The righteousness of Your testimonies is everlasting;
Give me understanding, and I shall live.

PRAYER

Heavenly Father,

You are righteous. Your regulations are upright and fair. You have commanded Your instructions in righteousness and great faithfulness. Thank You.

As I consider Your righteous instructions and Your great faithfulness, my passion for others to know You and obey Your instructions is overwhelming me. Help me to always have the right attitude, and express Your love and longsuffering through prayer and patience.

Your promises have been thoroughly tested. Thank you, Father. This is why I love Your word so much. Although I am insignificant and despised in the eyes of many people, I remember Your commandments are right; they are my delight. Your justice is eternal and Your instructions are perfectly true.

As the pressures and stresses of life bear down on me, let me always find joy in Your commandments. Help me to recall Your promises of old that have already been fulfilled. Let me never lose hope in Your word. Your laws are always right. Help me to understand them so that I may live a victorious life, know You and be confident in Your faithfulness.

Thank you for revealing truth and instructing me in righteousness through Your word.

I seal this prayer in the Excellent Name of Jesus the Christ and His Blood, and the Spirit of Truth, with thanksgiving. Amen.

Day 19

Hear My Cry, Lord

Have you felt as if God is ignoring you? You are persistent in prayer, petitioning and praising, but still no answer or deliverance from your situation. It happens. You cry out for help and make promises, as if to bargain with God. Sometimes it works and sometimes it does not. Always remember God works according His plan to bring about His purposes. In your distressful cry for God's help always stay focused on His faithfulness to watch over His Word to perform it in His timing and for His purposes. Keep crying if you must, but as you cry out, "Hear me, O Lord," keeping believing and declaring His commandments are truth and are eternal.

Verses: 145-152

145 I cry out with my whole heart;
Hear me, O Lord!
I will keep Your statutes.
146 I cry out to You;
Save me, and I will keep Your testimonies.
147 I rise before the dawning of the morning,
And cry for help;
I hope in Your word.
148 My eyes are awake through the night watches,
That I may meditate on Your word.
149 Hear my voice according to Your loving-kindness;
O Lord, revive me according to Your justice.
150 They draw near who follow after wickedness;
They are far from Your law.
151 You are near, O Lord,
And all Your commandments are truth.
152 Concerning Your testimonies,
I have known of old that You have founded them forever.

PRAYER

Heavenly Father,

It is because of your mercies I have not been destroyed; your compassions never fail. Thank you for new mercy today! Great is thy faithfulness to me.

Hear me, Lord! I pray with all my heart; answer me, Lord! I will obey your decrees.
I cry out to you; rescue me so that I may obey your laws.
I rise early, before the sun is up; I cry out for help and put my hope in your words.
I stay awake through the night, thinking about your promise.
In your faithful love, O Lord, hear my cry; let me be revived by following your regulations.
Lawless people are coming to attack me; they live far from your instructions.
I believe that you are near, O Lord. I am confident that all your commands are true.

I have known from my earliest days that your laws will last forever.

Thank you for revealing truth and instructing me in your ways.

I seal this prayer in the Excellent Name of Jesus the Christ and His Blood, and the Spirit of Truth, with thanksgiving.

Amen.

Day 20

Rescue Me

What has been your plight in life after accepting Jesus Christ as Savior and Lord? I can say, unashamedly, that I have had my share of adversity. Like Job, every area of my life has been impacted. Thankfully, not at the same level of calamity as Brother Job. I must admit that there were times when I could not petition God on the basis of my faithfulness and obedience to His word. Nevertheless, He remained faithful and revived my spirit according to His word and His tender mercies.

Once again, the psalmist expresses his need for God's salvation—deliverance. Once again, he petitions God on the basis of and in accordance with His statues, judgments, and testimonies. His confidence in the mercies, loving-kindness, and truth of God's word is his leverage to petition God. Also, his love for God's precepts and his obedience to God's law establishes his relationship with God as well as his reverence for God. What a privilege to petition God based on your obedience to His Word. Meditate on these verses and pray accordingly. He will deliver you.

Verses: 153-160

153 Consider my affliction and deliver me,
For I do not forget Your law.
154 Plead my cause and redeem me;
Revive me according to Your word.
155 Salvation is far from the wicked,
For they do not seek Your statutes.
156 Great are Your tender mercies, O Lord;
Revive me according to Your judgments.
157 Many are my persecutors and my enemies,
Yet I do not turn from Your testimonies.
158 I see the treacherous, and am disgusted,
Because they do not keep Your word.
159 Consider how I love Your precepts;
Revive me, O Lord, according to Your loving-kindness.
160 The entirety of Your word is truth,

And every one of Your righteous judgments endures forever.

PRAYER

Heavenly Father,

Great and mighty God, it's another day that you have kept me. Thank you! I'm humbled by the privilege to approach You in the name of Jesus Christ my Savior and Lord.
Father, today I ask that you look upon my suffering and rescue me, for I have not forgotten your instructions.
Give me favor, O God; defend my case and preserve my life according to your promise.
Lord, great is Your mercy toward me. Revive me by following Your regulations.
Many persecute and trouble me, yet I have not swerved from Your laws.
I pray that I am not distracted by seeing the wicked disobey your law. I am sick at heart because they care nothing for Your word.
Your compassion, Lord, is great; preserve my life according to your laws. My enemies delight in

persecuting me, but I have not turned from your statues.
Let me not become bitter when I look at traitors with disgust who seem to prosper without obeying Your word. Look upon me and see how I love Your precepts, LORD. In your grace, revive me
The main thing about Your word is that it is true and all your just rulings last forever. I am confident in this.
Thank You for hearing my prayer as You promised.
I seal this prayer in the Excellent Name of Jesus the Christ and His Blood, and the Spirit of Truth, with thanksgiving. Amen.

Day 21

I Love Your Law

If you profess to be a Christian today, you are ridiculed. In some foreign countries Christians are persecuted and severely oppressed. I cannot say how it feels; I can only imagine by the reports I read. I would hope that my faith not fail and that my lips would still utter His praise. I would d like to think that my heart would still stand in awe of God's word.

Do you think you could rejoice at God's word if you were being persecuted without a cause, other than for being a follower of Jesus Christ? Read the verses below and meditate. Pray and make your declarations as the psalmist. Go ahead and express your love for God's Word in spite of the risk.

Verses: 161-168

161 Princes persecute me without a cause,
But my heart stands in awe of Your word.
162 I rejoice at Your word
As one who finds great treasure.
163 I hate and abhor lying,
But I love Your law.
164 Seven times a day I praise You,
Because of Your righteous judgments.
165 Great peace have those who love Your law,
And nothing causes them to stumble.
166 Lord, I hope for Your salvation,
And I do Your commandments.
167 My soul keeps Your testimonies,
And I love them exceedingly.
168 I keep Your precepts and Your testimonies,
For all my ways are before You.

PRAYER

Heavenly Father,

Great and mighty God, it's another day that you have kept me; thank you! I'm humbled by the privilege to approach you in the name of Jesus Christ my Savior and Lord.

Lord, I present my cause to you today…Powerful people harass me without cause, but my heart trembles only at your word. My desire is to obey your instruction; therefore my heart is afraid to disobey.

I rejoice in your word like one who discovers a great treasure.

I hate and abhor all falsehood, but I love your instructions.

I will praise you all throughout the day because all your regulations are just.

Thank you for giving those who love your instructions great peace and they do not stumble.

I long for your rescue, Lord, so I have obeyed your commands.

I have obeyed your laws, for I love them very much.

Yes, I obey your commandments and laws because you know everything I do.

Thank you for hearing my prayer as you promised.

I seal this prayer in the Excellent Name of Jesus the Christ and His Blood, and the Spirit of Truth, with thanksgiving. Amen.

Day 22

Praise and Delight

For all God has done the least I can do is utter praise. What a privilege to come before His presence to cry out to Him, to petition Him. More importantly, to acknowledge and confess that we have gone astray. Like the caring Shepherd He is, He receives us back into the fold. Yes, my delight is in the Lord and I will meditate therein day and night. I vow to never forget His commandments and I shall share His truths with others as long as I live. As long as I live, I will praise God and obey His instructions so that I can live here and now and in eternal glory with Him.

What about you?

These closing verses of this psalm emphasizes the psalmist's love for God's directions and his need of God's help and the transforming power of His directions.

Verses: 169-176

169 Let my cry come before You, O Lord;
Give me understanding according to Your word.
170 Let my supplication come before You;
Deliver me according to Your word.
171 My lips shall utter praise,
For You teach me Your statutes.
172 My tongue shall speak of Your word,
For all Your commandments are righteousness.
173 Let Your hand become my help,
For I have chosen Your precepts.
174 I long for Your salvation, O Lord,
And Your law is my delight.
175 Let my soul live, and it shall praise You;
And let Your judgments help me.
176 I have gone astray like a lost sheep;
Seek Your servant,
For I do not forget Your commandments.

PRAYER

Heavenly Father,

Great and mighty God, it's another day that you have kept me; thank you! I'm humbled by the privilege to approach you in the name of Jesus Christ my Savior and Lord.
O LORD, *listen to my cry, I pray; give me understanding and a discerning mind as you promised. Listen to my prayer and my supplication; deliver me according to your word.*
My lips shall utter praise to you, O LORD *because you teach me your statues.*
I will declare your word; I will speak of your word for all your commandments are righteousness.
I pray, let your powerful hand be my help because I have chosen your precepts.
Lord, I long for your salvation and help; your instruction is my joy!
Let me live again so that I can praise you! Let your rules help me.
I confess I have wandered off and strayed like a sheep, lost. Thank you for finding me. Help me to stay close, hear your voice and obey. Help me to never forget your commandments.
Thank you for hearing my prayer as you promised. I seal this prayer in the Excellent Name of Jesus the Christ and His Blood, and the Spirit of Truth, with thanksgiving. Amen.

Keywords Definitions And Phrases

Keywords and Definitions

଄ଃ

Hebrew Word Meanings

Commandments (Hebrew, *mitsvot*) – a distinct, authoritative order. Ex. "I do Your commandments" v. 166.

The word *commandments* is used 22 times in Psalm 119. Commandments pertain to anything the Lord God has ordered. The word indicates God's authority to govern His people. The commandments of God are positive and negative, specific and general, restrictive and permissive. However, most important, they help an individual to identify his or her way in this world, which is filled with confusion, error and sin.

Judgments (Hebrew, *mishpat*) – a binding law; judicial decision. Ex. "I will praise You…when I learn Your righteous judgments" v. 7).

This word *judgments* is used 23 times in Psalm 119. It is derived from the Hebrew word meaning "to judge." God has made decisions that are like the legal rulings of a judge in a court of law. He has made judicial decision on what is acceptable behavior and what actions will receive His blessing. If we make decisions that oppose God's binding decision, we endanger ourselves and others associated with us because of our unacceptable behavior. Because God is just, we can trust His judgments to be good for us. He is the judge over all; His decisions establish true justice.

Law (Hebrew, *torah*) - the first five (5) books of the Old Testament; the Torah, also the Pentateuch.

Ex. "So shall I keep Your law continually, forever and ever" (v. 44)

The word *law* is used 25 times in Psalm 119. The basic meaning is *instruction* or *direction*. If refers to all of God's instructions given to Moses. The law was given to the Israelites, whom God had established a covenant relationship. It was to teach them how to live as God instructed, that is holy. The Law of God, also called the Law of Moses, was for the people's good as revealed by God through His servant, Moses.

Precepts (Hebrew, *piqqudim*) – injunction; requirement; commandments. Ex. "I will keep Your precepts with my whole heart," v.69.

The word *precepts* is used 21 times in Psalm 119. The Hebrew word means "an appointed thing," "something for which someone is given charge." The word has the same idea as a commandment (v.4), because both words assume that the God who commands has the authority "to take charge" or "to appoint."

Statues (Hebrew, *huggim*) – things inscribed; enacted laws. Ex. "I will keep Your statues" v. 8.

The word *statues* is used 21 times in Psalm 119. The Hebrew word for statues refers to something marked out as a boundary, something inscribed or engraved. Therefore, this word speaks of the permanence of the Law. God Himself engraved it in stone (refer to Exodus 24:12). This same word is also translated "decree."

Testimonies (Hebrew, 'edot) – ordinances; God's standards of conduct according to the

Ten Commandments. Ex. "Blessed are those who keep His testimonies" (v. 2)

The word *testimonies* is used 22 times in Psalm 119. Its derivative is from the Hebrew verb meaning "to witness" or "to testify." It refers to the Ten Commandments, called the "two tablets of the Testimony" (Exodus 31:18). The commandments were a testimony because they were a witness to the Israelites of either their faithfulness or unfaithfulness to God's covenant (Deut. 31:26).

Way (Hebrew, *derek*) – the pattern of life required by God's law. Ex. "I have chosen the way of truth" (v. 30).

The word *way* is used 11 times in Psalm 119. More specifically, the phrase "Your way" is used and describes the will of God as a path that is distinguished from other paths, which lead to destruction. God's path leads to life; His ways are a reflection of His nature.

Word (Hebrew, *imrah*) – a general term for God's revelation. Ex. Your word I have hidden in my heart, that I might not sin against You" (v. 11).

It is used 39 times in Psalm 119. The Hebrew term for *word* originates from the verb "to say." The term is a general word for God's Law, encompassing everything that the Lord has promised and spoken. It speaks of all that God reveals, discloses or makes known. Also, it means the utterance of the Lord God.

Other Keywords & Phrases

Delight - The psalmist affirms and expresses his delight with the Law. This means he is committed his life on security of God's instructions. He values God's Law over material wealth.

Liberty - The psalmist says, "I will walk at liberty..." There is a freedom, but with boundaries set by God, that one has in obeying God's instructions. Although living according to laws and regulations is often misunderstood as limiting and restrictive, the Law of God is paradoxical freedom. It frees us from sin (v. 133), and gives us the peace that comes from following the Lord's instructions (v. 165).

Love - Throughout this psalm, the psalmist proclaims his love for the Law. He compares his desire to a thirst for water (v. 131) and a craving for honey (v. 103). Basically, his love and attraction to the Law is a result of his love for God Himself, his Teacher. If you love the Lord, you will love and obey His Word. They are inseparable. Jesus said, "If you love Me, keep my commandments" (John 14:15.)

"The wicked have bound me" - The psalmist uses this phrase to describe the hostility of a world in which rulers persecute him. He makes reference to his enemies fabricating lies about him (v. 69), and seeks to kill him (v. 87). However, note that the psalmist steadfastly proclaims his allegiance to God's law. He will not forget God's laws, precepts and testimonies even under pressure and the life threatening experiences.

This is the resolve all followers should have in this hour. Regardless of the hostile world in which we live, we resolve to obey God's laws and walk in the integrity of His Word trusting Him to protect us.

ᘓᘐ

ᘓᘐ

From the Author

I am sure you recognized that these were prayers, although classified as psalms (songs). They were heartfelt thoughts expressed by the psalmist. They clearly express that the Law of the Lord is this psalmist's delight. To him God's Law was excellent. Although he expressed concerned for his hostile environment and life threatening situations, he was steadfast in his commitment to keep God's law.

I find myself reading and meditating on Psalm 119 again and again. It enlightens me. I am able to see what my attitude should be concerning the Word of God. As I meditate on it, I can actually sense the Presence of God. It is like He breathes into my nostrils new life and elevates me to a place of rest in Him by thinking on His Word. Indeed, His Word revives my soul.

As Christians, we live in a hostile world. Our surroundings can pressure us to make decisions and choose paths that oppose God, but like the psalmist, no matter what challenges we face, we should always choose God's way.

I repeat like the psalmist, we all need God's help to remain devoted to Him and to His instructions, which for us, is the Bible. I pray these thought-provoking meditations and prayers have been a blessing to you, and has awaken your hunger and thirst for God's Word, directions and instructions in your life.

Exalting the Excellency of the Word,

Queen

Other Books by Queen Phillips

Cost of Commitment
A collection of poems and prose

Inspiring the Soul, Enlightening the Mind
A collection of essays and inspirational messages

Letters from Heart to Heart
A handbook on the letter writing ministry

Words Just for Women
Messages and sermons for women in leadership ministry

The Patriot Project
Poems in tribute to U.S. military personnel and veterans

Prayer Principles for Beginners (E-book & Paperback)
A resource to develop and maintain a consistent prayer life.

The Path to Promise (First Edition)
Moving Forward after Brokenness

The Path to Promise (2nd Ed., Paperback)
How to Move Forward after Brokenness

22 Days Prayer & Meditations: Psalm 119 (E-book)
A devotional of adoration for God's written instructions for life.

www.ingramcontent.com/pod-product-compliance
Ingram Content Group UK Ltd.
Pitfield, Milton Keynes, MK11 3LW, UK
UKHW020219250726
13967UKWH00001B/92

9 781304 639905